The Battle for

HEALING

HOW I LEARNED TO TRUST GOD AND FIGHT TO TRIUMPH OVER MY SICKNESS

JOHN MOUSER

HIGH BRIDGE BOOKS
HOUSTON

The Battle for Healing
by John Mouser

Printed in the United States of America
ISBN (Paperback): 978-1-946615-75-6

Unless otherwise indicated, all Scripture quotations are taken from the Holy Bible, New Living Translation, copyright © 1996, 2004, 2015 by Tyndale House Foundation. Used by permission of Tyndale House Publishers, Inc., Carol Stream, Illinois 60188. All rights reserved.

Scripture is taken from GOD'S WORD®, © 1995 God's Word to the Nations. Used by permission of God's Word Mission Society

Scripture quotations taken from the Amplified® Bible (AMPC), Copyright © 1954, 1958, 1962, 1964, 1965, 1987 by The Lockman Foundation. Used by permission. www.Lockman.org

Scripture quotations marked MSG are taken from THE MESSAGE, copyright © 1993, 2002, 2018 by Eugene H. Peterson. Used by permission of NavPress. All rights reserved. Represented by Tyndale House Publishers, Inc.

High Bridge Books titles may be purchased in bulk for educational, business, fundraising, or sales promotional use. For information, please contact High Bridge Books via www.HighBridgeBooks.com/contact.

Published in Houston, Texas by High Bridge Books.

Not only have the Mousers walked through everything mentioned in this book, but I personally watched them do it with incredible attitudes and unwavering belief in God's goodness. I pray that as you read their story you would believe that the same God that was faithful to them will be faithful to you! John effectively unpacks the reality that life is hard, but God is good! I'm confident that this book will meet you where you are and fuel your belief in God's ability to get you where you want to be.

—**BEN WARD**, Pastor at Gateway Church

For those of you who are unfamiliar with the name John Mouser let me tell you what I know firsthand of him. He is a man who hears from God. He is a man who has experienced a touch from heaven and now lives, leads, and serves with the fingerprints of God all over his life, family, and ministry. John is a man of devout and radical faith. There is no doubt that John's story will impact your life and that this book will douse kerosene on the smoldering embers of your faith. Get ready to go on an amazing journey and step into a new dimension of the healing power of God.

—**JOHN E. SKIPWORTH, JR.**, Lead Pastor at Rochester Assembly, Rochester Minnesota

Contents

Contents

This book is dedicated to my amazing, gorgeous wife, Christine, who never left my side, and our miracle son, Deacon Bentley, who was birthed at the end of this season.

Introduction

I'm an open book, so I always let my audience in on how the Lord deals with me—how he loves me, gives me grace, and shows me the path using the rod and staff. Your story may be different from mine, but that's ok. We only need one John Mouser running around on the earth. God has made each of us unique, so celebrate your unique ability.

I will never forget the following statement by Pastor Denny Duron: "A setback is just a setup for a comeback." This is the hardest book I have written thus far. I hope these pages challenge you to see Jesus with open eyes and to be willing to take the path he chooses for you as you pour out your heart to him. Please read this not with a religious mind but with a heart that God is a good, good Father who is madly in love with you.

John 10:10 says, "The devil comes to steal, kill, and destroy but I have come that may have to the fullest." Most of my life, I lived the front part of this scripture with my bad choices. Now, being a spirit-filled believer, I am living the last section. As you read, you will see this scripture come to light in a new way.

This book is for all the people who have been through the trials and believe God is still in control of making their life beautiful. As Jeremiah says in chapter 29:11,

"For I know the plans I have for you," says the Lord. "They are plans for good and not for disaster, to give you a future and a hope."

We look at our life and ask, does God still have a plan? Does he still care? Did I miss it? I hope as you read the pages of this book you would find comfort, direction, renewing, and refreshing from the Lord. I pray that I can encourage you on your journey wherever you may be. May your faith be lifted to the highest capacity so you can receive the fullness of what the Lord desires you to have.

This story is simply about believing for a miracle in the midst of tragedy. I've seen the look on the faces of fathers when they bring their son to be healed from blindness only to have to walk back to their chair empty-handed. The story told here is about a belief that just never gave up. Please be encouraged. I don't know when or where God will heal you, but I believe he wants to. I am certainly crazy enough to believe with you for miracles. I still believe our God is ready to do more miracles than we believe he can do for us.

1

Playing Jesus

This book began on a plane from Boston headed home after we spent a great Christmas vacation with my wife's family. I was just thinking and reflecting like always, and then I felt prompted to begin writing about the season of sickness I was walking through. Little did I know when I began this journey that I would write about one of the hardest seasons I have ever faced in my life as a young Christian man. This book would describe how God would use a major storm to cross me over to the next stage and purpose of my life. Mind you, I was writing a story with no good ending, but writing it gave me hope that God would indeed give me a happy ending.

Everyone pays a price for their journey. Pastor Rodney Duron from Shreveport, Louisiana had to pay a price to leave his legacy as a mighty evangelist who walked powerfully with the presence of God. He had opportunities to make lots of money but chose to live a life of trust and faith in God. He chose to accept God's call on his life for full-time ministry. The Bible discusses selling our soul to gain the whole world. This makes me think about devoting yourself totally to gaining power, money, respect, status, success, etc. At the end of it all lies emptiness if it's not done for a purpose.

It's like climbing the top of the ladder only to realize it was against the wrong building, or having all the power and money only to use it for yourself, or being successful only for personal gain. The impressive people are those put in a place of power who empower others; those who have lots of money but give away lots of money; those reach a certain status and help bring others up; those who want to be successful only to teach others how to be successful. The point the Bible is trying to teach you is to focus on Jesus alone and you will inherit all these things.

> Seek the Kingdom of God above all else, and live righteously, and he will give you everything you need. (Matt. 6:33)

You will have the heart of a giver, the heart of a leader, the heart of a servant. If a man loses his life for Christ, he will find a new life in Christ (Matt. 10:39).

The Accident I'll Never Forget

In 2012, I had no idea my life was about to take a drastic turn. I had a near-fatal encounter when my spleen was enlarged and then ruptured during a concert setup. I began to bleed internally, which had never happened before, so I didn't know the symptoms. After 30 minutes, I began to sweat. After an hour, I found myself in my own vehicle going blind from blood loss. I was simply trying to get fresh, cold air as panic set in, and I lost control of my body.

Shortly before I lost my sight, I reached out to my girlfriend at the time, Christine, letting her know something was wrong with my body. She felt the urgency of this message, thank God, so she searched for me. As I glanced up toward the church, I saw her coming my way, and then, boom, my world went black. I touched my eyes to make sure they were open, and they were. In panic, I yelled for her to pray for me, I felt like I was slipping out of this world, banging on the door for help!

The Lord impressed upon me to share this story from Christine's point of view. Her account is as follows:

> Our day began as usual for a Sunday morning; we would see one another at church before service started. I was serving on stage like I have many times. John actually had this Sunday off from serving and being his usual social self, going to see everyone. Little did we know what lay before us. I was running around handling things for service while John and I caught each other's eye from time to time.
>
> I then noticed he was sitting on a pew a couple of rows back from side stage. This caught my attention because, like I said previously, he was being his usual social self. There wasn't anyone around him and it was still early, so people hadn't arrived yet for church. We caught each other's eye and he smiled at me. When it was time for worship to begin, I had my serving team by my side.
>
> I was the director, so I was in charge of running the service.

I then received a text from John that read, "Something is wrong with my body." I immediately felt an urgency. I asked him where he was. I didn't get a response quick enough, so I turned to one of my guys and said, "I have to go check on John." He said, "We got it," so I then went off stage to the hall that led to the south foyer. He was nowhere to be found. I received another text saying he was in his truck. I knew where he normally parked, right outside the south foyer doors.

As soon as John saw me coming, he started honking his horn. I picked up the pace to get to him. When I arrived at the driver side of his truck, I saw that he had the air on full blast, he was chalky grey, and he was in a lot of pain. He was moaning and moving his head back and forth. I asked him what hurt, and he just kept pointing to his chest.

I knew I had to do something fast. I had my radio on since I was serving, and Shae was on the other end serving in the media booth. I told her I needed our paramedics team. She could hear panic in my voice and calmly responded with clear instructions about how to reach them on the radio. I then switched channels and said, "I need paramedics to come out to the south foyer to the parking lot for John Mouser." I heard nothing in return for what seemed like a long time but then I heard a man say, "Did someone say they needed paramedics?" I said, "Yes, south foyer, parking lot. John Mouser is in his black truck, hurry!" I had stepped away from John to radio my sister, so I was making my way back to him when speaking with our security team.

When I arrived back to John's door, he said, "Just pray as hard as you can for me!" I laid my hands on him and began praying. I then saw the medics running our way. Before they got to us, I looked at John just as he lost his eyesight. The glaze over his eyes was immediate. He instantly panicked. He was trying to grab things saying, "I'm blind; I can't see!"

When the medics arrived, one of our pastors came as well. I explained what little I knew. They could see the urgency because of his skin color. They brought up a crash cart and started an IV on John, and he began to see again. One of the team members, Johnny, was on the phone with 911 while this was going on. Thankfully, we could see the fire station from the parking lot. We were unsure of what was happening, but we knew he needed to get to the hospital fast. EMS arrived quickly, loaded him in, and then left in a flash.

I was still in total shock so I headed to the church to get my things so I could go to the hospital. I almost couldn't think straight. Since I was so upset, John's friend Miguel went with me. I knew I had literally stared death in the face that day.

That experience was the strangest thing. I could hear people, but I had no sight. Panic and fear set in hard. Was I really about to die? It had taken me 25 years to get to church—would I now die in a parking lot? As all this was taking place, I began to feel peace and rest and a still voice speaking and calming me down. I had a picture of open hands in my mind. It was like the Father in heaven was reaching out his very hands to let me fall into. I've never experienced anything that strong and powerful. I could feel the second heaven and earth in this very moment. I thought I was about to die, but I wasn't at all scared. I was just thinking, *Why so soon; I'm still so young.*

The medics were working to revive me, and my sight returned after the IV fluids entered my system. By then, there was a great crowd watching in concern. They pulled me out of the truck, laid me on the stretcher, and loaded me into the ambulance. Immediately, the medics began checking my vital signs. From the medic's perspective, the only sign I had was sweating and blindness.

I think about the blind man Jesus met. All he knew to do was to have Jesus pray for his sight. Little did he know Jesus was going to give him far more than just a new set of eyes. With spit and mud, he created a new life for this man. "Be made whole" is what Jesus told him. I was being made whole too, just in a different manner. My wholeness was being made on the inside, where it really matters. If the inside is whole, the outside will be made whole over time. Jesus knew if he could change people's heart, he could change their life, then that would change their family, then that would change the city, and then the world. I refer to this as a compound effect. Jesus always brought compound impact, compound influence to people and regions. One person Jesus encountered would run and tell others about their experience.

As the ambulance traveled to the hospital, the medic was putting the cords on my chest. He stopped and looked and found out I was bleeding internally. Then he radioed a medic code to the driver. The ride got bumpy then. He didn't know where it was coming from or how to stop it, and he had no blood to give me to keep me from bleeding out. I remember looking at the medic knowing whether I lived or died, I would be fine. The life Jesus had given me was far better than I'd ever had. I had truly experienced life. I knew who my wife was. I had forgiven my dad. I had been forgiven. I was watching my mom's prayers in action as God was transforming my life. The medic, on the other hand, was scared for me. I could see it in his eyes, but he did a fine job of calming me down and telling me I would be fine. I remember him keeping his hand on me. I wonder if he was calming me or if Jesus was in me calming him.

I entered the emergency room, and at least 15 people were there—nurses, friends, pastors, and medics. They were moving quickly to do tests to find the bleeding. I prayed, *Lord, give them the wisdom to find this bleeding.* I recalled in my truck having pain on my left side, so I said, "I think something is wrong with my spleen," and that's exactly what it was.

At this point, I was ready to get old-school ugly with someone because of the level of pain I was in. Suddenly, my lifelong friend John appeared and said, "Hey, man, I'm going to read you this scripture." And he read, "Your promise revives me; it comforts me in all my troubles" (Psalm 119:50). Even though I was at my breaking point, it helped me. I'm so glad to have friends like that.

I entered surgery in great pain but peaceful. Whether I lived or died, God had orchestrated great miracles in my life already. If I woke up from the surgery to face another day, I would see many great days and miracles ahead. As I awoke from the surgery that lasted a little over an hour, I remember feeling like a machine. Everywhere I looked there, there were tubes—down my throat, through my arms, through my nose, on my chest, and in my side. I was about to lose my mind. You would never know that I am claustrophobic, but if ever box me in, you will find out how bad it is. I have been in a few MRI machines and had to be medicated every time.

During a splenectomy, they make a zipper cut from belly button to mid-chest. They suction the blood and look for where the blood is pouring from. I had a hematoma that covered 70% of my spleen. They pulled the spleen out and then cauterized it, placing some staples or clamps on the main artery that ran to the spleen. To complete the surgery, they installed a JP drain to continuously remove the excess blood that was loose in my body. They removed a little over 800cc of blood. To help you see the picture, I lost one pint of blood. You need a blood transfusion when about two pints is lost. Dr. Kevin and his team did an excellent job and completed the surgery in a little over an hour.

The Recovery

I awoke in the Critical Care Recovery Unit. There I was full of tubes and strapped to a bed. I was processing all this in my head and seeing if I was okay, and then I looked down and my legs had casts on them. This pushed me over the edge. Just as I grabbed the tubes going down my nose and mouth, the nurse walked in.

"No, no, no, sweetie you definitely don't want to pull them out!" she said.

I mumbled a loud, elephant-like noise since I couldn't talk with a tube down my throat.

She said, "It will be okay, honey; I promise. You just hang on."

I could feel the tears running down my face, and I just wanted to scream. This was what an arm would feel like when you break it and a cast has to be put on it. I was broken and there was a proper way I needed to be cared for to recover fully. There is no shortcut. God has to take us through situations in different ways and seasons of our lives so we can heal.

I want to zone in on the story of the woman with the issue of blood. She had a problem and no one could help her, but she knew Jesus had the answer. When she grabbed his garment, he said, "Who touched me?"

What is happening on the inside is far more important than the temporary discomfort outside. I later found out there were 39 staples in my stomach and a JP drain out my side to remove all the excess blood from my body. This brought me peace.

I leaned over to my mom and said, "Open your Bible, and look up the story of Jesus when he was whipped."

Jesus was whipped with 39 lashes, and he had blood pouring out of his side. I thought to myself that this was a real-life experience of playing Jesus. In 2 Corinthians 11:24, it says, "Of the Jews five times received I forty stripes, save one." With my math, that's 39. Then John 19:34 says, "However, one of the soldiers stabbed Jesus' side with his spear, and blood and water immediately came out."

This was a divine moment for me that God would orchestra such a perfect and timely event. I felt so honored to go through such a trial. Being Jesus in the Easter production and then seven days later living it in a small way was an honor.

The doctor ordered me to rest as much as possible. I had 39 staples in my stomach, so I was fragile. All I could do was sit and read. I watched some TV, but that got boring fast. I read many books and listened to many podcasts during this time. It was miserable for me because I love to be active, be around people, and be productive. The healing process of laying around on a couch or a bed didn't make me feel productive.

Sarah Young's *Jesus Calling* devotional says this:

> Thank Me for the conditions that are requiring you to be still. Do not spoil these quiet hours by wishing them away, waiting impatiently to be active again. Some of the greatest works in My kingdom have been done from sick beds and prison cells. Instead of resenting the limitations of a weakened body, search for My way in the midst of these very circumstances. Limitations can be liberating when your strongest desire is living close to Me.
>
> Quietness and trust enhance your awareness of My Presence with you. Do not despise these times. Although you feel cut off from the activity of the world, your quiet trust makes a powerful statement in spiritual realms. My Strength and Power show themselves most effective in weakness.[1]

I did more than read that. I soaked it up and repeated it daily. I also tried to read the Bible as much as I could. Honestly, it was hard. I like to read and live it out. This season, I had to read and read and read and read.

> Be still before the Lord, all mankind, because he has roused himself from his holy dwelling. (Zech. 2:13)

> This is what the Sovereign Lord, the Holy One of Israel, says: "In repentance and rest is your salvation, in quietness and trust is your strength, but you would have none of it." (Isa. 30:15)

> But He said to me, My grace (My favor and loving-kindness and mercy) is enough for you [sufficient against any danger and enables you to bear the trouble manfully]; for My strength and power are made perfect (fulfilled and completed) and show themselves most effective in [your] weakness. Therefore, I will all the more gladly glory in my weaknesses and infirmities, that the strength and power of Christ (the Messiah) may rest (yes, may pitch a tent over and dwell) upon me! (2 Cor. 12:9 AMP)

David Wilkerson once preached and told the following story:

There was a lady who had taken care of her husband for a long time. The man was sick with cancer, so he had been through many treatments. The husband told the wife, "This cancer has stolen my life. It has robbed me, and you will never know how that makes me feel."

Well, the wife, of course, had something to say. She said, "That cancer stole from me too. I couldn't live my life; I had to take care of him every day, every night." Be aware that what happens to her, happens to you.[2]

This made me think about how my family has helped me so many times. There are few people I thought about immediately—Pastor David Yonggi Cho and Watchman Née. Pastor Dewitt had told me at the hospital to look them up. Pastor Cho went through a difficult season with tuberculosis. Then one day he gave his heart to Jesus and was miraculously healed.

Romans 5:2-3 says,

Through Christ we can approach God and stand in his favor. We brag because of our confidence that we will receive glory from God, but that's not all. We also brag when we are suffering. (GWT)

I stopped right here. Okay, you may brag, but I'm not bragging yet. I thought, *Lord, how can I brag about uncontrolled pain and sickness that nobody understands?*

When someone comes to the cross of Jesus, they really began to live. Matthew 10:39 says, "If you cling to your life, you will lose it; but if you give up your life for me, you will find it." It's only when we lay our plans, our desires, our dreams, and our lives at the feet of Jesus that he can resurrect our broken, messed up lives into a beautiful story. You see I found life in every cross I had to carry. Whether it was waiting for the right time and season or letting sickness propel me into more of his abundant life. We can't define life the way we always have. We must define it the way God's Word does. We have a plan to win the world, but if God's not in it, then what's the purpose. I want to be where God is.

I previously said that when giving your life to Jesus, then and only then will you find your life. I want to share from the heart how difficult that was for me. I had never accepted any wisdom or listened to anyone my whole life. When I met Jesus, I felt his wonderful love, mercy, and presence in my life in my darkest hour, so I gave my life to him over a period of time. Jesus was the only one loving me in that jail cell that day. For the first time, I began to let people direct my life to line up with God's Word. I wanted to keep his love, mercy, grace, and presence flowing freely in my life. There also was this rest and peace in my soul I always longed for. I had all the monetary things before, but I was never satisfied, nor did I possess any peace or rest. 2 Corinthians 4:17 states that "our present troubles are small and won't last very long. Yet they produce for us a glory that vastly outweighs them and will last forever!"

---

[1] Young, Sarah, "February 16," *Jesus Calling,* 49, Nashville, Thomas Nelson, 2004.

[2] "Trusting God with All Your Tomorrows by David Wilkerson," YouTube video, 49:06, "SermonIndex.net," April 10, 2014, https://www.youtube.com/watch?v=hEAEopnCzeM.

2

The Struggle

With no spleen in place, my body was in safety mode. If I inhaled any chemicals, I would be sick for the entire day. There is no more humbling sight to see as a man than your wife mowing the grass because you couldn't—the one who vowed to be the caretaker, provider, handyman, grass mower, and vehicle maintenance man. My role had taken a shift, so as I got out of the car, I just went inside to wash the dishes and do laundry, something I knew I could do. I wanted so badly to complain and be resentful toward God for allowing this sickness to take place. I wanted to have a Louisiana hissy fit in the kitchen that day. Even in my lack of understanding, I said, "God, I believe that you are good and that everything has a purpose. I'm not seeing much now but time will tell what's really going on."

As I thought about how Jesus commands us to love the church as he did by giving his life for it, I thought to myself *I don't feel like I'm serving her very well.* Christine is such a champion. She always told me how thankful she was for what I have done for her. As I received these messages, I felt hopeful that God was working for my good. Because of the picture I painted in my head, I had thought marriage would be different. Have you ever painted a picture and the results were way off? This has happened to me every time. I'll begin on what I think is the journey God has set me on and then everything begins to fall apart. Proverbs 16:9 says, "We can make our plans, but the Lord determines our steps."

The choice I faced was to either keep going or quit, and I would not allow myself to quit. I've found that I learn a lot about myself and who God is in these journeys that don't go as I planned. I got to the other side thinking, *Man, I'm different having gone down that uncomfortable, seemingly insignificant path.* I believe the paths have brought me more into submission and understanding of what God's path looks like to fulfill his will for my life, when things are going not my way but his way and I'm not in the driving seat of control but the passenger seat of humility. I began to write as I struggled through these tough seasons. I didn't want to complain, so writing helped me vent my emotions while keeping my attitude positive and spirit hopeful.

When seasons like this come, we normally go to the Word, desperately seeking a similar situation to relate to. We always seek to feel human by instinct, but there are rare occasions when God wants to do a new thing in the earth through his creation. For this to take place, he must find a willing and submitted individual. I believe God knows there will be times where they will want to quit, give up, turn back, and run far away. He knows when they reach that point the real work of the Spirit is being done to the greatest degree. God makes a way when there is no way.

At a recent home group gathering, a leader shared this powerful story that just flooded me with joy because of the season I was in. She said, "Think about King Hezekiah in the Bible. He was a man of God, and then he became deathly ill." I mean, he was pleasing to God. He was faithful. He wasn't seeking to be rebellious toward God or live in compromise, but sickness came. Just before this happened, the previous chapter described how the Lord sent an angel to destroy 185,000 of his enemies. I thought God was probably happy with him. I wasn't sure if that would happen for me, but I would be encouraged if that was where the sickness started for me. Maybe the Lord would just send another angel to heal him.

The rest of the story picks up in 2 Kings 20:1. As soon as Hezekiah got sick, immediately, the prophet Isaiah visited him for a not so encouraging prophecy, to say the least. He said, "Put your affairs in order; you're about to die—you haven't got long to live." The next verse sent chills through my body. It was like the Lord was there in my room. As I write this, the tears fall down my face over and over. Verses 2 through 3 say,

> Hezekiah turned his face to the wall and prayed to the Lord, "Remember, Lord how I have walked before you faithfully and with whole-hearted devotion and have done what is good in your eyes." And Hezekiah wept bitterly.

Our finite minds can't understand God's ways, what he sees, and how he makes his perfect will come to pass in our life. I remember when all this started, I had no word from the Lord on the season of sickness. I was left to put trust in the gap for the first two years. Let's see what happened to Hezekiah after he had a much-justifiable meltdown. Verses 4 through 6 say,

Before Isaiah had left the middle court, the word of the Lord came to him, "Go back and tell Hezekiah, the ruler of my people, this is what the Lord, the God of your father David, says: I have heard your prayer and seen your tears; I will heal you. On the third day from now you will go up to the temple of the Lord. I will add fifteen years to your life. And I will deliver you and this city from the hand of the king of Assyria. I will defend the city for my sake and for the sake of my servant David."

The next section of this story is where I was fascinated. As the leader of that homegroup described this section, it was like a thousand lights came on in me.

Meanwhile, Hezekiah had said to Isaiah, "What sign will the Lord give to prove that he will heal me and that I will go to the Temple of the Lord three days from now?"

Isaiah replied, "This is the sign from the Lord to prove that he will do as he promised. Would you like the shadow on the sundial to go forward ten steps or backward ten steps?"

"The shadow always moves forward," Hezekiah replied, "so that would be easy. Make it go ten steps backward instead."

Isaiah the prophet asked the Lord to do this, and he caused the shadow to move ten steps backward on the sundial of Ahaz.
(2 Kings 20:8-11)

God, who created the sun, set into motion how it would operate, and declared it good, went back into the genesis account to adjust things for this man just so he would have the confident assurance that God would heal him, even after God had spoken through his prophet. It gets me so fired up that he would even defy his own laws, his own principles, his own creation, just to give confirmation to one man. What makes me laugh is this isn't the first or last time he does something like this. There is another story in Joshua where he stops the sun. God must really care about us knowing that he listens to our prayers. That helps me know how important it is to God that we get what we need to go on. He is such a great God and such a great savior. Just take a moment to thank him for helping us.

As this season progressed, I was reading a lot and looking for answers. But there were no answers, just a long, quiet time to trust that God was still good. I ran across this from Rick Renner's "Sparkling Gems Devotion."

We tend to use this word "plague" to describe worldwide pandemic outbreaks, but that is not the way it is used in Mark 5:29, which tells of a woman who had an issue of blood for 12 years. Specifically, Mark 5:29 says that when this woman touched Jesus, she was healed of her "plague." Yet this woman's sickness was not contagious, nor was it imminently life-threatening, since she had been sick with it for 12 years. So today I want to tell you about how I discovered the meaning of the word "plague" in the New Testament and why this was such an important discovery to me...

So what is a "plague" as it is referred to in Mark 5:29? It is an ailment, sickness, or affliction that regularly strikes an individual again and again. It is a recurring condition that is not serious enough to kill but that continually keeps the individual sick and miserable. It is a sick, demented, elongated devilish attack upon an individual's physical body that causes discomfort and pain. Thus, this word mastigos, translated "plague," would describe chronic conditions such as migraine headaches, rashes, allergic reactions, high blood pressure, foot fungus, and so on. These are conditions that come and go, can last for years, and rarely permanently respond to medication or the treatment of physicians...

Medicine is an important tool in administering aid to physical suffering. However, throwing medicine at a spiritual attack can at best bring only temporary relief; the symptoms will inevitably come back again because you are dealing with an attack and not an entirely physical problem. This was a great revelation for me, and it resulted in my physical healing. I stood up to each attack and resisted it in Jesus' name until those recurring allergic reactions stopped. The power of Satan that was attacking me was literally broken, and I've been free ever since.[1]

I believe the devil attacked me with a plague. Some days I would be sick multiple days in a row, so I read the word and prayed for hours. Then I would erupt into preaching and then switch to thanking God for how good he is. In my sickness, I thanked God.

Did you hear me? I always wondered if that was the reason for this season—for me to develop under pressure and unfortunate circumstances. I needed to cooperate with God. I believe God forms great things on sick beds and prison cells. As I've said before, let's think how God thinks. That is the theme of this book. When major trials come, we are getting ready to be made greater, stronger, and more compassionate for his people. The harder we get hit, the stronger and more powerful we become and the more authority we carry. Like the Bible says, we must be thankful in all things—good or bad.

After three months of recovery, I was so glad the doctor released me to go back to work, although returning to work caused many health issues. This was a tough adjustment. I got sick a lot during this time. I had no idea that losing my spleen would cause sickness my body. To me, it seemed like my body went into protective mode. My dream career seemed to be going up in smoke with my new reality. I was frustrated at this stage of the recovery.

At one point my boss, being a longtime friend, sat me down and told me there would be a change in my position. They needed me there every day to paint and help with the production of the team, but my sickness was causing me to miss several days a week of work. I told my boss I wanted to pray about the next decision and get back to him in the next few days. I needed some time to listen and rest.

Let me share some things about rest that I reflected on during this time. Contrary to popular teachings, God desires you to enter his rest, as discussed in Hebrews 4. He chooses which way he wants this to take place in your life. Joyce

Meyer says this will bring major spiritual warfare. I believe I entered a season of consecration through this season of sickness.

One year the Lord told me to rest, and all I could think about was how I wanted to be on the move for Christ. Do, do, do is all I had known. Believe, then act, and serve was the gear I operated in for many years. Also, my temperament was to be around people constantly. I get energy from being around people. I normally trusted in my skills to get where I needed to go, but my skills wouldn't help me in this season.

I began to see the number 44 everywhere. On my clock, every day I would either hear or see 44. I started reaching out to others to see if they knew what it meant. I had a few great ideas, but none really stuck with me. Then after a few months, as I keep looking, asking, and wondering, one of my mentors suggested I read Psalm 44:1. It said that they entered the land without their strength. So just like I felt my skills wouldn't get me to the next stage, this number and scripture said the same thing. I believe God was saying, "Trust me in a new way, trust me without your human strength, trust me without your skills, trust me to do what only I can do."

I remember working on a car and I had a twisted bracket in the vise. This bracket was all out of shape, so, of course, I had to beat it back straight. The Lord said, "John, this is what I do to you sometimes. Your tendency is to get out of whack or bend one way, so I have to reform you." This will never be comfortable. I was in a place I couldn't change for myself. Only God could get me out. No doctor could understand what was going on. I couldn't run away anymore because I was so far into relationship with him. I knew far too much about Jesus and he had developed me so far and I didn't want to ruin all that he had done. The contrition began. Diamonds go through a very similar process.

What Do I Do Now?

The Lord asked me to step away from my job at the Toyota dealership. The day I left my job, I went home to seek the Lord. In just two weeks, he performed a few major miracles. My bankruptcy was canceled, so they sent me a large amount of money claiming I overpaid. Then the day I finished my first memoir book, "From Addiction to Addition," my friend emailed me that he was starting a publishing company. The very next day, a close friend said he would build me a body shop. I just needed to send him the address to send the materials. As my shop was being constructed, a friend allowed me to work for him. That was a little too divine to just randomly happen. When my friend emailed me about the publishing company, I knew God was calling me into a new season of being a book author.

Once my shop was completed, my business began to bear fruit. It wasn't super busy, but it was steady. I could work for him and do my shop on the weekends. Juggling the two started to get a little tough, and his business was growing, so I stepped out so others could help take it to the next level. About a week after I was back working for myself, my compressor quit working. I bought another one to finish the customer's car, but the next weekend I had the same problem. I researched and found one for sanding and painting cars. I picked it up, got it all hooked up, and then had the same problem. Then my transmission went out the same week and the first compressor quit working, so my work truck went to the shop.

I was having a lot of trouble sleeping at night. I thought it was because of the pollen and my allergies adjusting to the weather. When I called my customer to tell them it would take longer to finish their car, I felt this weight on my chest. I had to let go of control of my life. I wasn't intended to be in the driver seat. I texted the electrician to see if he could figure it out. I went home and just said, "God, I have no answers; I have a lot of questions but just no answers. You are probably trying to tell me something and I'm sure I've missed it. I will not talk to another individual until I hear back from you." I laid on the bed waiting for him—no phone, no music, no TV, no book, no Bible—nothing.

Finally, I began to feel the peace of God. I started wondering why I pushed myself so hard? Was I trying to be somebody I wasn't? I remembered the Lord saying to me through my friend Gabe, "John, when you rest in me, I reign. When you reign, then I rest. The Lord can do more in a second of you resting in him than you can do in a lifetime of trying to do it yourself." Man, this rocked my world. I had always been a go-getter. I was fast-paced, busy, driven, and passionate every day. I couldn't see wasting one second or waiting for somebody else to help me. I always did what I could with what I had. The Lord was saying cease from movement, but this might have been the hardest thing I've ever tried to do. If my body is still my mind is still moving 100 miles an hour. I began to just do what was needed. As I laid there on my bed, I drifted into a wall stare and it was great. I was being lazy, and it felt good not to be multitasking for a change. Here's a little encouragement I read days before from one of my mentors:

Psalm 23:1-2. The Lord is my Shepherd; I shall not want. He makes me tie down in green pastures; He leads me beside the still waters.

For those that have an issue slowing down in life — mentally thinking to yourself, "I'm trying to slow down" is an excuse to make our conscience feel better so that we can keep moving fast.

Just slow down, then do it. It will feel as though we are losing money, being lazy, or falling behind, but in reality, we are putting ourselves in the "following" position behind God so he can help "lead" us into His purposes and prosperity.

If we are ahead of God leading Him, we cannot sufficiently hear what He is saying. All we hear is what "we" are saying to God.[2]

Believing in Miracles

As I went through this little trial, it was difficult to go meet the Lord. I normally woke up a little early to read, pray, and worship just to be with him. It always makes a great day when I am with him in his presence. One Friday morning, I sat on the bed and said, God, I'm frustrated with you and I don't want to be." I realized how this trial had affected me and my relationship with Jesus. I've been through many trials, many tough seasons, but they had strengthened my faith. This time was different. I had been shaken to my core. I wasn't as strong as I thought I was. How humbling is that? It made me think about how arrogant Christians can be. I felt like I was ready for anything. I would pray, "Lord, search my heart, mold me into your desire, teach me your ways." that is what he did, he just didn't do it my way. For every difficult situation in my life, he has turned pain into purpose, a mess into a message, but he always did it his way.

Proverbs 3:5-6 says,

> Trust the Lord with all your heart, and do not
>   rely on your own understanding.
> In all your ways acknowledge him, and he will
>   make your paths smooth. (GWT)

I was having trouble trusting the Lord. And I wondered how long I had been trusting in myself and my ways? My mentor Ben always used to say you can't do God's thing your way. Well, I've sure tried to repeatedly. Without meaning to, by default, I resorted to the three-year-old mentality, mine, mine, mine.

Isaiah 26: 3 says,

> People with their minds set on you, you keep
> completely whole, steady on their feet, because
> they keep at it and don't quit. (MSG)

This was what I clung to because on the inside I felt I was losing my mind. I felt like my confidence was gone, my peace was gone, and my joy was gone. Where did it go, though? My focus had changed somehow. Things that were once priority had become common. The Lord was teaching me again to seek his face. I felt so weird through this time in my life. I didn't feel like myself. It was difficult. I wanted to be normal so badly, but I knew something was happening. I just couldn't put my finger on it. Only in his presence would I feel better.

A few days later, after we took a weekend off to rest, I woke up to the sound of a doorbell ringing repeatedly. When I answered, no one was there. I said, "Uh oh, Jesus must be knocking at the door of my heart. I sat back down and said, "Lord, help me open the door you are knocking on." My mentor Mickey said, "John, the Lord has an open door he is about to show you."

Somewhere in my Christian walk, I had become a lot like the Laodicean church. I thought everything was going pretty well in business and taking on this new season, but the Lord desired me to go after him more. He desired me to be hot on his trail, not just when it was convenient. I thought I was wild for Jesus, but God says, "Come up higher." We are far more desperate for God than we may realize. When we are in a trial, we seek him through prayer and the Word, but when things get better, we usually slack off. We must continually push in to him daily, weekly, always getting closer to him to know him better and better.

Relationships with people are similar. We notice someone, start talking to them, visit them, and perhaps eventually commit to being with them forever, but the pursuit can never slack or stop, or the relationship begins to die. The same is true for our relationship with Jesus. Smith Wigglesworth said, " If you are in the same place today as you were yesterday, you are a backslider." It all boils down to how much you give him, how hard you pursue him, and how desperate you are to see his plans come to pass over yours. I have had the conviction that if I'm not as in love with God as I was when I first met him, I'm a backslider. Over the years, I have done some sliding, but I have also done some climbing. At the end of the day, my goal is to be as close to Jesus as I can and being as welcoming as I can to people who don't know him.

There is a liberating Christian life full of freedom out there for us. What will we let get in our way? Here is a glimpse of the treatment we will receive if we truly operate in all he has given us. In Revelation 3:7-12, it says,

> Write to the angel of the church in Philadelphia: The Holy One, the True One, the One who has the key of David, who opens and no one will close, and closes and no one opens says: I know your works. Because you have limited strength, have kept My word, and have not denied My name, look, I have placed before you an open door that no one can close. Take note! I will make those from the synagogue of Satan, who claim to be Jews and are not, but are lying note this, I will make them come and bow down at your feet, and they will know that I have loved you. Because you have kept My command to endure, I will also keep you from the hour of testing that will come over the whole world to test those who live on the earth. I am coming quickly. Hold on to what you have, so that no one takes your crown. The victor I will make him a pillar in the sanctuary of My God, and he will never go out again. I will write on him the name of My God and the name of the city of My God the new Jerusalem, which comes down out of heaven from My God and My new name.

When the Lord of the labor commands you to rest you rest. You have been commanded to rest, be still, wait, cease from striving, cease from sowing, cease from serving, cease from all activity and focus on him only. Rest and waiting are more focused for intentional reflection and to become awestruck again like the first time you met him. Seven is the number for rest and the number of completion or perfection. Most people feel like if they aren't busy busy busy, they are not productive. With the Lord, it's different. In one minute of your rest, he can do what would take you a lifetime. When you rest in him, he reigns; when you reign in control, he rests. Somebody will have the reigns—either you or God. It seems like an easy choice, but most choose to reign in control.

When I began to have health issues, it was frustrating. The allergic reactions gave me migraines, so I couldn't move. I got sick so often I would just lay in agony. I hated to be still and held down. I felt like I was losing my mind. I shared this with my wife and just wept. She prayed for me, and then we went on with our day. Every time I took medicine, it paralyzed me for most of the day. Some days it helped, but most days it was just a Band-Aid. There were no answers everywhere I looked. People would pray for me, but I would just listen. I'll never forget being at a friend's house and I felt the Lord speaking to me about my sickness. He said, "I took you into the season to prepare you for your destiny." Wow. I could think of 100 different ways to do that, and this would never be close to that list.

One night I attended an Ignite America Conference and the man grabbed the microphone. He said, "Jesus asked me seven years ago to wait on him." He spoke about the process he went through in learning how to wait on the Lord, being silent, and being still. I knew it was more confirmation of the reason for the season I was in. At times, I was bitter at the Lord for the pain and hopelessness I was experiencing. I felt I was missing out on life—birthdays, friends, accomplishments, events. At heart, I am an evangelist, so being still and having to be restrained is like tying up a two-year-old child. You can imagine the frustration. If you are sick, be encouraged. Jesus Christ wants to heal you.

Matthew 8:17 says, "He bore our sickness and disease." Your pain has a purpose, your sickness contains significance, your agony is an agent of impact, your feelings of death are bringing destiny. There were times I felt bedridden and was so filled with depression and gloom. You may have wanted to take your own life because of the pain and suffering of your illness. I, too, thought about such things until I figured out that I was going through this for a reason. I was in the valley to help others one day move from the valley to the mountaintop when my healing came.

You see, God would rather send one of his people to help others out and bring them through their struggles. When there was a sin problem on earth, he sent Jesus. His love doesn't make sense. It's like sending your child to a war zone just to get one kid out of the line of fire. He desires that no one should perish having not experienced his love, salvation, and hope.

A friend once asked, "John, you losing weight?

"Yes," I replied, "not on purpose either. I am trying to gain weight."

Then her fiancé told her about my sickness. She said, "The Lord's plan for you is not sickness." *Here we go again with the awkward conversation of my sickness.* You almost become defensive when people speak to you like you don't believe in healing. I know God has great plans for me, but I lost an organ serving him. Now I'm always the topic of prayer and sympathy. I try to stay low key about my condition because everybody always made sure I knew God is a healer. My two cents is I've probably talked to God a time or two about this, and we have both agreed this isn't forever. Later in the evening, she asked if she could pray for me. I'm always down for prayer, so she prayed and afterward said, "Be sure you haven't made an agreement with the enemy and that you're not bitter toward God."

Okay, well, you try serving God in an Easter production, nearly dying, and then have to walk through a super-long season of utter chaos and physical limitation. It aggravated me, but I knew this was the Lord trying to help me, so I smiled and thanked her. I felt like the Lord was asking me to quit rebuking this season and let it serve me. Sometimes you just say it's better if I just keep my mouth shut and thank God for his goodness. That's a real word there. Just keep your mouth shut and thank God. I felt like I didn't have the faith that God would heal me after being in the season so long. I know I did though. I wanted to make sure I hadn't gotten too comfortable with it. I didn't want to make friends with my sickness though. Days went by when I would simply push through, even though I would cry through the pain, weariness, doubt, and feelings of defeat.

Standing on the Word

I turned to many different people the Lord highlighted for me. One of them was a Christian rapper and author, Pastor Trip Lee. This was a very encouraging connection. I knew he didn't always understand what was going on, but he just keeps on going. He wrote a song that nailed the wood to the wall called "Sweet Victory." I'll share some of the lines I found so real and profound.

> You see me limping;
> I know you see me limping.
> You can't tell on the CDs,
> but, bro, I'm knee-deep in it.
> I'm wading in my weakness;
> He made me dependent.
> I'd be lying through my teeth
> to say I don't resent it.
> Even as I write these lines, I'm close to tears;
> my body ain't been working right for seven
> years.[3]

It floored me to hear another person say what I felt inside. Then he said,

> You don't know my life boy,
> you don't know my life boy,
> you don't know what it's been like on my wife.
> Don't know my fight boy.
> Been in them trenches steady,
> trying to fight my foes,
> and when I could fight no more,
> He brought me low, low.
> He brought me low.
> I know I can't bear that load.[4]

I've heard this song a million times. Still, to this day when I hear it, I weep. There is something about lyrics and music that communicate so much more than a tune or noise. It's a heart speaking. If you can ever write what your heart is speaking, you will never have trouble connecting with people, whether they are hurting or happy.

Another story that gave me hope is Luke Smallbone's from the band For King and Country. He talks about the season of sickness he went through with ulcerative colitis. Here's what he says in an interview: "If you gave me a choice to redo the last few years of my life and eliminate my struggle with illness, I'd choose to walk through it all once again, because today I send this message to you as a man more full of joy and hope than ever before. Sickness has transformed my perspective on life, marriage, God, and music." He and his wife Courtney sang a song together called "Without You."

I believe God uses people to help us through our seasons, but there is nothing like directly hearing his voice. When you have heard God speak to you personally, something inside of you yearns to hear it again and again. After cultivating a lifestyle of tuning into the Lord's voice, it makes it difficult to hear sermons from other people. I listen to pastors I know because I desire to get the impartation of wisdom and hunger for Jesus. The only sermon you want to hear is the one the Father in heaven is preaching. We all need to have a voice in our life, whether it be a pastor, leader, mentor, or life coach, to help us stay humble and accountable but hearing God speak for yourself is exhilarating.

Try it now, if you dare. Just close this book and say, "God in heaven, I repent of my sins. Open my heart and ears to hear you speak. Now wait silently until you hear him, no need to rush. I promise it's worth the wait. Your mind will take a while to slow down to silence, and then you will hear him whispering to you. You will feel like time is standing still and then a calmness will come over you. There is nothing like Father God.

I often think about what it must have been like to be Jesus. He had no control over his life but was controlled by our Father in heaven. Let's look at a few stories. In Matthew 4:1, Jesus was led by the Spirit into the wilderness to be tempted by the devil. In the previous verse, he had just been obedient to his Father and to the current process in that day and age. God had opened the heavens and said he was well pleased with Jesus.

Many times, we find ourselves in situations we can't control or fix. I believe they are put there to teach us how to manage what we are given—good, bad, or ugly. Whatever season we are in, we need to manage it well. We need to hold our heads high. Maybe it's sweeping the stage off when we have the gift to be a world-class actor. Having little control is the best way to ensure you will travel the way the Father intended you to. If you get to your platform in life too fast, you will make it all about you.

Maybe it feels like hell or is agonizing, but, nonetheless, it's what has been prescribed for your process. I never wanted to write books. I never took classes to learn to be an author. The reality is the Lord asked me several times to write a book about my story and I consistently ignored him. Then when I finally did it, my life fell apart, so I thought. The day I finished the manuscript, I lost my job in the career path I had been on for close to 16 years.

If you have ever been through a lengthy illness, you will relate to this paragraph well. When people asked how I was,

I was tempted to tell them, but I knew they would then make cliché statements or have pity on me. So I responded, "Just fighting the good fight." I wanted to be treated normally for a change. I have feelings and want to be myself even though I'm going through sickness. I think too often when we are around sick people, all the emphasis is on their condition and not on who they are.

I am all for miracles of healing, but I also know God has called many a person to walk through difficult seasons in life. Sick people need friends who will care for them, not just take care of them. You can still laugh when you get sick. Life goes on. It doesn't have to become your identity. It's just a pit stop or a gas station you're passing through and then you'll be back on the highway of life with a new perspective in no time. You could be a secret weapon for another time as you are pioneering through difficult times. You could be God's answer to help others overcome their obstacles. God desires that we help our brothers and sisters, whether they are Christians or not. Love trumps anything.

What if healing has a path?

What if your healing isn't instant like it has been in the past?

What if you have to go through the dark valley to get equipped with more power, authority, character, and humility to share with your brothers and sisters on the mountaintop of victory?

You see, the mountaintop is not just about your victory, but it has to be shared with your brothers and sisters as encouragement, refreshment, and hope. If you can understand not everything that happens is about you, then you can start building the kingdom of heaven selflessly. When someone gets a promise fulfilled, it does something to the body of

Christ. It sends a shockwave of excitement. It makes people leap with joy. Praise fills the mouth and heart of those who watched the process. Celebrations happen. Either way, whether healing comes or doesn't come, God is still good. Even though you're sick or can't move, reach out through email, text, etc. The Lord will you use to touch people even though you're down.

David said God teaches him how to war. He cried out, "Deliver me, oh, Lord, I'm about to fall. Deliver me. Bring me out of this." You are going through what you're going through because you asked God to do something big in you. You hold people up through your prayers and if God takes you out of the war, they will fall. He needs you to go through this battle to lift your brothers and sisters up. I wanted out of my sick season many times. I screamed to God for many days. I would go weeks being sick. Day after day I was so sick I couldn't even talk. I would just put praise music on and cry. This is battle. We were built for battle. We were built to bring strongholds down and lift the name of Jesus high. Some days I would be sick and say, "My body is filled will power from heaven to destroy any sickness, addiction, and depression. No weapon formed against me will ever prosper."

Here's the Bible's definition of suffering.

> Before you made me suffer, I used to wander off,
>   but now I hold on to your word. (Psa. 119:67)

> I know that your regulations are fair, O Lord, and
>   that you were right to make me suffer.
> (Psa. 119:75)

Imagine what David was going through. Was it sickness, was it loneliness, was God testing him? At different seasons, it was probably all three. The Bible declares that God is the same today as he was before. I believe he lets us go through things to teach us.

My sick season contained rare allergies that were mostly misunderstood—from food to activities. It could have made me be bitter at life and God. In my painful dark hour when I had a reaction, I could easily complain, but I just worshiped him. He gave me life. He knows the answers. He knows the end from the beginning. I let my weakness drive me to worship. It's easy to be a believer when life is going well, but the true test is when life falls apart. Only then can you see what you're made of. It's not rocket science, either mud or rock? Pal, I'm going to build on the rock. Even if I'm sick at times, I have Jesus with me. All of heaven is constantly surrounding me. I have peace. I have rest. I have his presence. I have salvation. I have his love. I have his freedom. I don't have it as bad as others. Let the falling rocks push you closer to Jesus. Let them help you trust him more. Let them make you more desperate.

I was driving down the street one day and began to get sick and couldn't figure out what was causing it that day. Normally, I would just endure and get over myself, but I was a little testy. "God, how does it make you feel to watch me go through this?" I asked, and not nicely either. He said, "It makes me feel the same way I felt about Jesus when I watched him be beaten, whipped, dragged, and then crucified on that cross. I knew there would be far more glory than there would be pain." I was speechless. I felt like a jerk too for being like that toward God. It made me respect him and want to worship him more in times of sickness, when I normally wanted to complain.

> I form the light and create darkness, I bring prosperity and create disaster; I, the LORD, do all these things. (Isa. 45:7)

God will use pain to create a love relationship with His creation, but this may challenge your theology. Let's go to the Word and open up some of the tough seasons God allowed to build the mighty men of God that have gone before us.

Consider that God allowed Jesus to experience incredible pain to create an opportunity to have a relationship with his creation. Consider how Jesus created a relationship with Paul. He blinded him and used a crisis in his life to bring him into a relationship with him and use him for God's purposes. Consider how God recruited Jonah for the mission He had for him.

The process of a calling begins with you following Jesus, not leading him. When you lay your carnal thoughts down, you can walk in your calling. The process will require much prayer, much worship, much fasting, much obedience, much warfare, much fighting, much travailing, and much weeping, to name a few. As you draw near to him, he will draw near to you. The process of a calling will require much sacrifice. You will have to lay down what you want so you can find out what Jesus wants you to do. You have a dream and God has a dream. Which one are you seeing daily? Who do you think about all day? What are your priorities every day? Do they have to do with healing people, building his kingdom, preaching his gospel, seeing people born again and delivered? You will either serve God or serve yourself, but you can't do both.

Ask yourself daily whether the cross will be a decoration or a life-giving source. Will the cross remind you of how you received a new life or a trendy addition to the house? For Jesus, the cross was his destiny—it represents the purpose for which he came into the earth. It wasn't pretty either; it was heavy, full of blood, sweat, and tears. Make sure your image of the cross isn't just decoration but a reminder of the cost Jesus paid to give you a new life.

One day I was journaling, and here's what I wrote that day. Recently, I was in a tough spot, having all kinds of troubles—health, business pressure, financial stresses, and marriage stresses—and I felt I couldn't find God's presence. I read, worshiped, prayed, witnessed, and loved people, but it seemed Jesus was playing hide and seek. I always first check myself when I get like this. Usually, I've missed something, disobeyed somewhere, or I'm being tested.

I thought, *I will just wait here and ask the Lord to come and help me.* I didn't have a lot of strength, so I was desperate. I wanted to be a true seeker, so I said, "Jesus, you have been so good to me and my family. Even if you never show up, I'll still come here to meet you. Even if I never feel you, even if I never hear you speak again, you have given me more than enough to worship you in the short time I've known you." There is a song I love to listen to by Vertical Church Band, and it goes like this: "If I have you and nothing else, I have everything." Isn't that the truth? If we can just zone in on him, nothing else stands a chance.

When I'm focused on him, I can feel the transformation happening in me. When I focus on other things, they lower my faith, they lower my peace, they lower my pursuit after

Jesus. I just sat there and waited on God. It was so exciting. I had never just waited on him. I had only just begged him to show up. There is something about waiting on Jesus to come. He doesn't have to come and do something for you; he is free to just come and be. There was so much appreciation birthed in my heart for who he is and all he does for us. This waiting made me weep, and I'm not even sure why, I wasn't upset, I was just thankful that I knew help was on the way. I knew when it came, it would be awesome. Waiting helped me trust God and that his ways are for my good.

I've found that life is not a place or achievement but long walks, small talks, moments with people you love, helping others who could never pay you in return, having little money but lots of fun, being creative because you're on a budget. Life is the moments you are alive, sharing it with others. Life will never seem perfect but will always be what you make it.

When you have heard God speak, you won't have to go hear anyone else preach. You will only want to hang out with the Father. Why listen to someone else hear from him when you can do it yourself. I like podcasts, but I certainly would rather hear God speak directly to me.

In Philippians 1:15-20, Paul is speaking about the gospel going forth no matter what situation he is in, whether prison or death. I feel the same way, whether it be my former addictions, my experience from walking with Jesus daily, my many failures, or my allergies, the gospel is being preached.

Often, the Lord asks people to play hurt. You may be going through a season of sickness, a season of healing, a season of confusion. You may be battling being wounded by a fellow believer. The worst thing you can do as a Christian is lie down in defeat or take a break. Doing so forfeits your

DNA, inheritance, and ability to access the power and resources needed to overcome the battle. If you're fighting, God will give you the power needed. If you lay down and give up, then you have said, "God, we lost this one." In the Bible, there are tons of stories where the odds were stacked against armies, but God was on their side, so they were victorious. If you go to a battle without God, you are setting yourself up for total failure.

---

[1] Renner, Rick, "What Is a Plague?" Renner, last modified July 27, 2017, https://renner.org/what-is-a-plague/.

[2] Brad McClendon, "I Live Too Fast and I Can't Slow Down!", Living Vine Ministries, accessed September 20, 2019, https://livingvineministries.org/i-live-too-fast-and-i-cant-slow-down/.

[3] Trip Lee, featuring Dimitri McDowell and Leah Smith, "Sweet Victory," by Dimitri McDowell, Gabriel Alberto Azucena, Joseph Ryan Prielozny, Natalie Lauren Sims, and William Lee Barefield, in *Rise*, Reach Records, 2014, https://itunes.com.

[4] Ibid.

3

The Faith Step

We began hearing the Lord call us to move into the Dallas area. I had always thought about having my business there. It's the only place that made sense for such a large car operation. As we felt the nudge, our mentors were also transitioning from Shreveport to McKinney. McKinney is right outside of Dallas, a thriving area. I had been feeling the call to move for about a month, so I began to look at properties for the shop. I didn't have any loans, credit, or a stored-up ace in the hole—just faith in God, a wife, and a set of skills.

One morning at church, my pastor asked me, "John, are you guys going with Ben and Melandy to McKinney?"

I replied, "It has crossed our minds. We are praying to see if the door opens."

We agreed to seek the Lord to go with them and help plant a church there. I was so excited I couldn't even contain myself. For two years, I had been running my business by myself and with the help of my family. It was a blast doing that, and if we moved it would mean walking away from all that I was familiar with and all that had been built over the years.

In Genesis 12:1, the Lord said to Abram, "Leave your land, your relatives, and your father's house. Go to the land

I will show you. I will make you a great nation, I will bless you, I will make your name great, and you will be a blessing. I will bless those who bless you, and whoever curses you, I will curse. Through you every family on earth will be blessed."

Let's take a closer look at this passage compared to my life. This was the Lord's first promise to Abram, and it was the Lord's first promise to me. He promised me one night at a homelife group that I would have a body shop.

Upon his arrival in Canaan, Abram did not find a welcoming party and a brass band. "At that time the Canaanites were in the land" (Gen. 12:6). Other people owned what God had promised.

This story is interesting to me because the Lord told Abram to go and he would lead him as he went. We had taken a few weeks to seek the Lord, and I knew within the first few days that we would be going. We received confirmation after confirmation. My wife and I had a meeting with our pastor and told him we were indeed going to Dallas.

He said, "I'm am excited about this. It will be a great choice for you guys."

I was hoping for this great plan to come from him, but it was just more confirmation that we were on track. I'm a big-time faith guy, like blow your mind type. I do, however, get nervous when there is a major move happening and we are uprooting everything we know. God told Abram, "Go and I will show you. This would be a new level of trust for us. When the Lord asks me to do something, he usually has something else for me to step into.

When the Lord asked me to leave my career of 16 years of painting cars to follow him, I at least had a new book to sell. However, a new book is actually an expense more than it is passive income. We were pretty much in the same boat at this point. Abram's journey started from Ur—his hometown—and moved to Haran, to Shechem, to Bethel, to Egypt, to the Negev, to Bethel, to Hebron, to Mamre, to Dan. As he went, the Lord spoke to him. Abram never stopped traveling once he left his hometown. He traveled the whole time until he died at age 175. He stayed in a few places for a while and returned to some places twice. The more I thought about this, the more excited and nervous I became. Should I show Christine this story? Maybe I should wait. Both of us moving away from family and friends was probably enough right now.

I read something interesting in my Jeremiah Study Bible:

> It has been said that, for Abram, the symbol of his life was a tent, but the secret of his life was an altar. The tent spoke of his pilgrimage, of the fact he never owned the land. There were times in Abram's life that he moved from place to place. There were also long periods of time where he lived in tents in the regions of Hebron and Beersheba. But only rarely do we read of Abraham living for a time in a city. The altar speaks of his fellowship with God, for it was the focal point of his worship.[1]

Leaving the Nest

As we were adjusting to this new season, we had lots of fun conversations. Emotions were high, stress was trying to creep in on us, and we were forced to be in prayer to stay alert and enjoyable to be around. The more we sought God, the closer it brought us to hearing his thoughts. This may have been the greatest part for me. I have always desired for Christine and me to both be so thirsty for Jesus at the same time. I was in the first week of my two-week session of seeking God, and I heard him say for the second time that he would choose new venues to provide for us in this new season.

Oh boy! I was thinking he wanted to use the book or public speaking to show us new forms of provision. Pastor Denny and Mickey had both confirmed in the same week that the Lord wanted to use a different key to open this next door. Usually, provision for us looked like accounting or paint & body. We accepted it and received by faith what he wanted to give us. This takes me back to a vision I had the other day. I saw a picture of a huge canvas, which represented our lives. I then saw myself standing to the side watching, wondering what was being made. God was painting as I was watching.

There will be seasons and times in your life that you will have to do as I had to do in this scenario. I had to watch God as he designed what he desired. You see, I didn't know what he was trying to make. I had a good idea, but the more he painted, the more lost I became. In life, we naturally want to be part of the creation, and we add things like a little bit of blue or a little bit of red or a little bit of purple to help God paint his picture of our life.

Maybe we say, "God, do it like this or build this side up to make it look like this." All this is great if you, in the end, stop and wait until he finishes the painting to see what he wants to do and what his specific desire is for our lives. Think about how great of a designer God is, how he paints life when there is so much death. Be fascinated by how he works through people to lead you out of pits you have fallen into. Wonder at his plan for your life individually. He wants to set you free, put a brand-new identity in you, and set you among the kings in the earth.

Malachi 2:5 says,

> The purpose of my covenant with the Levites was to bring life and peace, and that is what I gave them. This required reverence from them, and they greatly revered me and stood in awe of my name.

The adjustment to not painting cars and just reading my Bible was hard, especially the first two weeks. I was excited about his new path to provide for me, but I was also nervous because there was no model to look to.

I began to write sermons and teachings about my life to have ready when the time came. I could hear the Lord saying, "Wait on me and rest in me." I would catch myself seeking new ideas or methods. This was far more obvious now that I was being asked to trust and wait on his opportunity and timing. I was at total peace when I was praying and thanking the Lord for taking care of our needs. We were in need, no doubt. I would soon need money to pay bills. My air conditioner also went out in my truck the same week. I needed a newer vehicle, which would mean another car note. I said, "Lord, you have got to breakthrough for us."

As I was looking for answers to my many questions, I ran across a sermon from Jentezen Franklin in his series, Spirit of Python. He said you know you're under attack when everything starts going wrong at the same time. He had my attention. He said you also know if you're under attack when all this stuff is overwhelming you into a corner and if you don't make a move, your ship will sink. I was definitely leaning in now. I even turned it up. He finished by saying you know you're under attack when you're physically tired or exhausted and have no desire to seek God or his Word. I was convinced!

I had been sick off and on for two weeks and had to force myself to seek God also. My thoughts lately had been, *How in the heck did I get here.* We had been planning for great and mighty things to happen and had been giving and praying like crazy. What was the deal here? But God certainly knows how to accelerate us. It's like a surprise birthday party that you can sense is being planned but they blindfold you and drive you there. Anticipation just kills me. I almost have to calm myself down before I take off the blindfold. I believe God does this for us.

I hoped the Holy Spirit would give me a clue about what was about to happen. You know how you question all your friends trying to get the inside details about something coming up. Maybe there are changes at work and you're trying to find out if you're on the "being canned" list. It's our nature to wonder and be curious when we don't know. I love being surprised, but I hate having to wait a long time for it. It's more than edge-of-my-seat entertainment. It's like I'm out of my seat jumping up and down trying to see what's going on.

Back to our transition—we traveled to McKinney to look at housing and check out the area to see what the Lord was saying to us. We found out this place was a major hot spot. People were pouring into the city faster than they could build buildings to live in. We planned to get all our ends tied up in Louisiana so we could make our transition in about a month.

When we returned, I attended church as usual. The house of God is an important place for me. There, I have learned how to serve, give, fight, pray, worship, preach, and live out the gospel. I've always made it a priority to be at the house of God for the preaching and teaching of the Word of God. I was setting up coffee for the pastors in the ready room and began speaking with this couple who were traveling pastors that came to lead worship for our church. As we talked, the Lord answered some of my questions through them. This got my attention. They were helping me trust God with their stories of God showing up right on time to pay their bills as they preached and traveled from church to church.

The guy found out I wanted to donate my books to prisons and preach there. He slipped me a card and said, "I can get you into any prison in Texas; I'm also a chaplain." I looked at his name and would you believe his last name was McKinney? I freaked out. No way, man. God is so desperate for us to hear him. We just have to be patient and pay attention. This was super cool for us because at one point it seemed like the McKinney plans were coming to a halt.

Christine and I found out we were pregnant with our first child, so that changed our perspective a bit. We began to feel like we might be pushing the Lord's hand to get over there, so we decided to wait and rest in his time. When I went to work at my shop, I said, "Lord, I love doing this— waking up, meeting my customers face to face, being relational, and then repairing their vehicle in a timely fashion and seeing the smile on their faces. I turned my focus on spending time with him and taking care of my current responsibilities and household in Shreveport. Work began to flood in after those two weeks. It's like the Lord orchestrated that time to have me sit and listen to him.

When Christine said she was pregnant, the testing began. This was why I was laying on the couch sick with a migraine. I was happy but wondered how I could be a dad. I couldn't even take care of myself. My chronic illness was unpredictable. We were in a tight spot vocationally and financially. I fought so hard my independent spirit of taking matters into my own hands. I always pridefully thought I could provide better and quicker than God. Though I never voiced that, my actions showed it. This time was different; I couldn't just go out and get a job. It would be just a matter of time before they noticed my attendance issue and let me go.

I was once again being broken before God. I would lie on my face and cry out, "God, what am I doing wrong? Help me, God; all I want is to do your will. Why can't this be easy? My testimony is strong enough; can't we just get on the easy highway?" Who taught us this Christian walk was easy? Just when I think it's about to get easier, then, bam, it gets tougher. God was offending my mind and showing that my heart was trusting in worldly systems, comfort, and security. I was broken, repenting for being a worshiper of idols and safety, and then being prepared to do two brand new things at once. I couldn't even pray sometimes; I was so desperate for God. "Help me not make a mess; help me follow you," I prayed.

As if that wasn't enough, I found out our insurance wouldn't cover the pregnancy. Oh, joy! At this point, I had no encouraging news. I struggled not to get mad at God. We were supposed to go to McKinney, but we had no jobs there, no house there, and my A/C went out in the truck in the summertime in Louisiana. "God, what are you trying to do? Help us see your plan in this."

Who you think God is will always be tested through fire. I have gotten to know God through every trial I've faced and every valley I've stumbled through. I've known God as Savior when my life was so filled with sin and he applied his blood sacrifice to make me a new creation. I've known God as deliverer when I was so bound by addictions and mindsets and he stepped in with his truth and opened my eyes to his love. I've known God as healer when he has brought me several healings in my body. I know God as provider when I lost my job and he sent me several thousands of dollars to build my own shop.

I came to know God as Provider when our insurance went up $500.00 a month and we were short $400.00 a month. He sent a miracle right on time as always. He has also shown up when we had steep credit card debt and Christine was pregnant. When we were moving to Texas to start a new business, he sent another man of God to cover all the bills as we began our journey. His body works best together. When we help one another and pray for one another, God has full reign in our lives to do what he desires.

Before we left for McKinney, Pastor Denny had said God may use me in full-time ministry instead of the paint and body shop, so I should be open for both. That went along with my thoughts that the Lord would use new channels and open new doors. I believe there will be many avenues or keys the Lord uses to provide for us how he chooses.

Several times, I felt like I needed to study for full-time ministry, so I got all my life messages together and studied the Word of God in my alone time as much as I could.

A man who was like a second dad to me said about McKinney, "I see you as a stallion in the spirit, I see the Lord holding your reigns and saying hold, hold, hold, then he says release! And when he does, you run like the wind! Release is coming!"

As we approached McKinney, we prayed and laid our thoughts down so God could move. It wasn't easy. The day I was scheduled for an interview to be a manager at an automotive service, I got a horrible migraine. It was so bad Christine had to pick me up, put my clothes on, and take me to urgent care. There I was waiting for the doctor to give me some medicine when the migraine disappeared. Christine told me she had people praying for me, so I texted each one that I would put them in a group for each time I got sick.

A few days later, I left the shop to have lunch at Subway. I arrived a little early, so I texted my wife, "Hey, I'm here." I felt my nose run, so I wiped it and saw that it was blood. Immediately, I got up and the flood came as I walked to the bathroom. In the bathroom, it was pouring out of my nose and then started coming out of my mouth. I couldn't get the towels fast enough. I looked in the mirror and thought, *Oh, man, you're about to die in the Subway bathroom. No way. Not me.*

I called Christine and said, "You have to come get me; I'm bleeding badly." I started to feel lightheaded, so I walked out of the bathroom, with blood everywhere, and said, "Please call 911. I'm bleeding and I can't get it to stop." I sat down in a chair and tried to lay my head back, a lot of help since it started pouring down my throat then. I felt something run down my throat like a chunk, so I got up to spit it out and it was a huge blood clot. That shocked me and another guy that had been watching me.

He then got up and said, "Let me get you some more paper towels." My wife pulled up after just a few minutes and at that same time, the fire department pulled up. My wife started cleaning me up and the firefighters gave me a cold pack and a gauze to stop the bleeding. After about three minutes, it was slowing down and then began to stop. Wow, I was so glad they recommended I get checked outside. I had never had a nosebleed before. My dad was having surgery that day, so I had Christine drop me off at the hospital with my mom just in case the bleeding started again. I had no more issues that day, but when I went to bed, I felt this fear grip me. What if I start bleeding in my sleep and don't wake up? I started praying until I felt it lift. Then I finally passed out.

When I woke up, there was no blood at all. Great! The bad news was I had another migraine. In the past month, I'd had 16 migraines—two weeks straight. I was so tired of being sick. The next day I woke up and the Lord said, "John you need to fast, you are being attacked by the enemy." I started fasting, just drinking liquids, until I got victory over again. After a few weeks, I had no migraines, praise God.

I went to Ben's dad's lake house on July 4th. We enjoyed a great weekend of fishing and being poolside. One day we were out on the lake and a plane landed in the lake. It was an old seaplane test running for the July 4th plane show. We happened to be behind it when it took off, so all we could smell was plane fuel. Another thing that made me terribly sick with migraines was the smell of fumes. That evening I felt it coming with the pressure, so I went to lie down. Ben and Melandy came into our room to pray for me. They said, "John, we believe the word of the Lord that today, this ends." As they prayed for me, I began to feel relief, which normally doesn't happen, for whatever reason.

I calendar everything I do because I forget easily with my short attention span, or ADD; call it what you want. As I reviewed my calendar and noticed I had pasted up one prescription refill date. The medicine I have been on for migraines is not so good for the body, so they only allow 15 pills over a 30-day period. If you get a lot of migraines, 15 pills are nothing. I used to refill the script on the 20th, but I made it to the 7th of the next month without medicine. That was extreme progress.

After praying daily, I had to cast off unbelief, fear, and doubt and believe God would make a way for us to begin a new life in McKinney. When we found out Christine was pregnant, it didn't change my mind but just added to the odds that were already stacked against us. We had only lived in our house for a year, so selling it would be tough. Someone had built me a brand-new shop just two years ago, and my customer base had been built for nine years just to reach success in a business I would be abandoning. The city we were moving to didn't want body shops due to their picky ordinances. Christine didn't have a job lined up nor did she desire to work since we were about to have a baby, and we didn't want to take our new baby to a new city and leave him in a daycare.

Houses are twice as expensive, and I didn't have an investor to borrow money to float me until I got on my feet. There were tons of odds stacked as high as the heavens, but we knew God was asking us to go. Only God could take care of all that. As I muddled through daily thoughts of how impossible it was, I began to violently declare, *God is faithful; his Word is true. No matter what gets in the way, he will blow the doors off!* I was listening to Pastor Denny one night and he said, "When we begin to move, God begins to move." What if we said, "God, I'm going to take a few steps and believe you? Do you think that's smart or risky? I think it's risky, but I think it gets God so excited. God says he is crazy, he believes me too much, he just jumps at the sound of my word in an impossible situation. I wonder if God is caught off guard by crazy faith. I wonder if he has thought, *Oh, my, they just jumped out into an impossible situation. If I don't save them today, their ship will sink.* What if we were people who don't even consider the odds or impossibilities. What if we acted as if our Father owns the whole earth? What if we walked that way and bowed to nothing, declaring that our Father owns this land? So if he says I can move here, then you will give it to me for free, because my daddy God owns it. This land, all these houses and buildings are my inheritance. I can use them however I want. That's bold faith. Be careful with bold faith because it can get you in trouble too.

A week later we found ourselves in a place we didn't see coming. My workflow had come to a halt—no new jobs, no phone calls. This meant bills were still coming in that needed to be paid. I began to remind the Lord that we were tithers, givers, children of his covenant. I believe that was my way of dealing with the worry and fear. Praying has always helped me work through my emotions and fears. Once I got past the selfish prayers, I was able to move to the more important ones, like asking God what he wanted to do here, what we needed to learn, and what his heart was. I stood back and realized I never focus on what his heart is. That made me sad. I'm supposed to be a Christian, AKA little Christ.

Maybe God was taking us through this to show us where our hearts were. Sadly, our hearts were wrapped up in what we needed, what we were thinking, what we were feeling, etc. I read a *Jesus Calling* quote by Sarah Young that touched my heart and made me see my daily walk with Jesus differently. It said,

> There's no need to wonder whether or not you are going the right way. I am the Way. As long as you stay close to Me, you are sure to be going the right way. Don't worry about what's on the path up ahead. Just enjoy walking with Me today.[2]

John14:6 says, "I am the way and the truth and the life."

Wow, I hadn't even stopped to think about that yet. Most of the time, I was thinking, *Take the smoothest road possible.* Sometimes Jesus says this is the road today. We say, "No way. That's not the Lord," but it very well could be. The Bible over and over tells stories where his people were led into seasons of hardship to grow, develop, and be molded. My battle in this season of slow-paced activity, of no full-time job, no real direction on how to get to the promised land, no real major activity going on was, of course, everyone's struggle—to simply rest.

Often, if you're like me, you get so focused on tasks that you can lose sight easily of taking a breath, enjoying where you are, and finding contentment in the now. I feel the seasons I've grown the most are the hard seasons, unfortunately. I've learned to be thankful in plenty and in lack, as Philippians 4:12 says. I would always draw near to the Lord, to try to get us back into a more comfortable season, but as I sought him, he would open my eyes to all I was missing around me. He would show me, "John you are living every man's dream, you married the girl of your dreams, you wrote a list of what you desired and you're married to that girl, you're living every addict's prayer of walking in freedom, every business owner's thought process where you run the business and the business doesn't run you, and you actually enjoy your career instead of despising it. You can't wait to get to work when most dread going. Wake up, son." I would then feel bad for trying to rush out of these hardship seasons.

Can we just say aloud God is such a good, good Father? He sits us down and just has a heart to heart talk. His talks to us always clear up our minds, hearts, and confusion. Let's pray that God would deliver us from these empty mindsets, that Jesus is closest to us when everything is perfect. Things will never be perfect.

I know your reading but let's have a moment to pray: Father, we need you to rewrite our thinking today. Help us see, whether we feel like we are in a good place or bad place, that you are with us and that all we need is you. You have resurrection power if we need that, you have hope if we need that, you have power if we need that, and you have love and peace if we need that.

During the first part of August, the Lord began waking me up at 4:00 a.m. When it first happened and I couldn't go back to sleep, I wondered, *What's the deal?* I went to the living room and laid on the couch. After about an hour, I went back to sleep until about 8am. The next day the same thing happened. Now I was a bit puzzled. I lay in bed trying to go back to sleep. After a miserable attempt, I got up and went back into the living room. I asked the Lord is there someone I need to pray for? Do you just want to love on me, or am I missing something?

I had this thought run through my mind: *Someone is at the door of your heart, will you let him in?* Then I started to cry. Obviously, this was Revelation 3:20. This little process was making my mind go crazy. If you ever try to make reasonable sense with your relationship with God and the things he does, you will be confused often. I tell myself a lot, *Yes, I feel stupid,* which confirms I'm doing what I should be doing. When it seems you have very little going on in your schedule, there seems to be a lot of God activity around you. The less you're active at times in your life, the more God can be active. The more you remain in a dead state, the more alive he can be in your life. The more your agenda is on the cross, the more you will find Jesus (the way). The Bible says we are crucified with Christ so that he may live. When you rest in him, he reigns. When you reign in yourself, he rests. Remember that. When you have done your portion of the partnership, you must leave it to him to do his. You can't help him do his part. Your mind doesn't need to understand, as long as your spirit is communing with God, that is the only matter of importance.

Lots of times we do what we think is our duty or responsibility and expect results. We have seen it happen like this for years. If I tithe then, boom, I get blessings or financial overflow. If I give a big gift away, of course I will get a big reward, whether it be financial or material. Well, since we are clear on that, what happens when you do all these things and nothing happens?—when you give, when you tithe, when you obey, when you fast, when you pray, when you worship. What if nothing happens. Will you keep doing it?

Christine and I went through a long season where we did what the Lord asked, but all we saw was more struggles, more budget pressure, more stuff started breaking, health issues. It was totally opposite of what you would expect. For six months, we pondered whether we should keep on doing the same things we had been. Our marriage vow was to be like Christ and make him known so we couldn't stop what we were doing.

Watchman Née writes in the book, *The Spiritual Man,*

> For anyone to pursue the Lord, he must oppose his own desire. If anyone wishes to maintain a true spiritual course with God, he must put to death his own desire. Those who cannot submit themselves to God's time are unable to obey God's will.[3]

This was not the section of the book I wanted to read. We live in an impatient day and age. We want what we want now, and we will do anything to get it. Sometimes that means leaving the Lord to do it. I believe he loves us so much but since we have free will, we can choose to wait on him to move or try to make it happen ourselves. In this season, I felt like I had been on both sides of this coin. I've waited as long as my flesh could tolerate and then I've I jumped up and tried to make it all happen.

There is a fine line between you doing your part and trusting God to do his part. See, when it's your move, you have somewhat control over the task. When it's God's move, you can kick, scream, beg, cry, and complain, but he doesn't budge. He always knows the best way in the best season and timing. I see many people struggle hard here, even abandon the Lord as I once did. They want it their way, in their timing, meeting their expectation. I've seen people blow past red flags just so they could get their way. I call this the "mine mentally." Everything is all about them, what they want how they feel, what they see—you get the picture. Then, somehow, they say the Lord did this or that. I always want to burst out laughing and say, "Naw, friend, if the Lord did that, it would look and smell like him from every angle. We have a natural inclination to force things into happening, thinking it's what we want, but then a few weeks or months down the road, we are no longer satisfied. It's called an illusion. We thought something was something that it wasn't.

My spirit always told me if I live at the feet of Jesus and stay at the foot of the cross, everything I need for my purpose, destiny, calling, etc. would find me. You see, there is a theology that if we don't do anything, nothing will happen. I believe God is so big he does not need our help. I also believe he desires our partnership, thus making us have a small portion of responsibility. My key in this section is to make clear what I've come to learn. Our little part is to obey in faith. Sometimes we get so busy we run red lights, but God put them there to save us from making messes or getting ourselves involved in stuff that wouldn't help us get to our destination he has for us. Yellow lights are meant to caution us. We should be aware and alert while proceeding. Then when you have a green light, you can go forward, focused on your destination.

You would think with all we have been delivered from, we would trust him, but we don't. God has trouble finding people that will trust. Our countenance will show if we are trusting God.

Are you full of peace, joy, rest? Why do you look like your God is dead when you walk around in public? Turn that frown upside down. Put a smile on your face daily. Where is your joy? We have too much to be happy about. What I've learned, and am still learning, is to listen to God and let him handle it. Do what you can do and let him work it out. Cast your care upon him and leave it. Relax. He won't work on your timetable either, so cool it.

David said, "My soul trusteth in thee." In front of a lion or bear, he trusted in God. In Psalm 42:11, David was cast down. He was seeking God; he wasn't in sin at this time, but his soul was cast down. He was weeping and praying, but something was wrong.

I've been here before. Tons of problems came in my business one after the other with the transmission and compressor. God was teaching me to trust him. David couldn't get it. He said, "God is trying to do something in me. Deep is calling to deep inside of me to bring me to a place of trust."

God desires to have a people who have learned to trust him. The waves won't sink you and the fire won't burn you; you give up trying to figure things out and surrender to his will. He is interested in you surrendering to his will, and then the calm begins.

Trouble never comes one at a time. I bet you could list a dozen right now. David was being dealt with. He used to sing, but he became impatient with God. He said, "Where are you, God. I prayed and sought you. Every one of us knows what that's like. But nothing happened. There was a spirit of impatience in David that God wanted to deal with. David came to the end of his faith.

Have you ever gotten mad at a fast food place for being too slow? I mean it's fast food. You want now food. God has a way and he doesn't apologize. He knows when and he knows how. You can cry and beg, but he is in control. David said to his soul, "You will hope in God." He was reminding himself that God was faithful and always came through. I have to do this daily. God, help me remind myself of your faithfulness.

When I'm trusting God, there is a calmness in me that is good for my health. You must settle it; live or die, you are the Lord's son or daughter. Even if you have to live in a tent, as long as he is with you, you're going to be fine. If you don't trust God, it will bring a curse on you. It offends God. Unbelief kept Israel out of the promised land. This sin grieves God. This causes pride in the flesh.

The Bible says you have need of patience after doing the will of the father, that you might receive the promise. If you're impatient, ask the Lord to help you. In Jeremiah 17:5,

> This is what the Lord says: "Cursed are those who put their trust in mere humans, who rely on human strength and turn their hearts away from the Lord."

This is running at it trying to make it work, manipulating, trusting the flesh, telling God you know best—that he is taking too long, making phone calls. There is a curse that comes from taking matters into your own hands. It's a dryness, emptiness. Check your intentions when you are doing something. If God told you to do it, get going. If he told you to wait, then wait. If he hasn't said anything, keep praying, keep asking, and keep knocking. I did this when God didn't bring me a mate soon enough.

The Lord says he will plant you. Those who believe God will always produce fruit and be watered by the Holy Spirit. The river will always water them. Pastor David Wilkerson said,

> There is nothing more dangerous than sharp minds making plans without God. They call it marketing. You better make sure you're led by the Spirit and the Lord is guiding you.[4]

Quietness and truth are your strength. You will be relaxed. God is taking care of it. Asa was a man of faith. He was outnumbered, but he trusted God. He cried to the Lord; he didn't have a plan. He declared that God was his God. Then God did it. Are you impatient about God's s breakthrough for you financially, in your marriage, or in your health? What is it you need but you don't see it? Your faith may be wavering, causing you to be dry and empty. He wants you to bear fruit and be filled with joy for his plans.

Ask God now to bring rest to your soul and that you will not try to figure it all out. I'm praying it with you. Take all these burdens off our back; help us to enjoy the lives you have given us. Let quietness and trust be our strength.

I once heard a story that a little boy went to heaven. Then they said, "What did you see? He said, "I saw Jesus there and Jesus played baseball with me." I believe that. I believe Jesus wants us to enjoy him and delight in him. Psalms says to delight your heart in him and his ways. That will bring rest and peace. Come and lay your unbelief, worry, and stress at the altar. Let him give you new faith. Lay that burden down; his yoke is easy and his burden is light.

Psalm 86:1-3 says,

> Bend down, O Lord, and hear my prayer; answer
> me, for I need your help.
> Protect me, for I am devoted to you. Save me, for
> I serve you and trust you.
> You are my God. Be merciful to me, O Lord, for I
> am calling on you constantly.

Let him be king, Lord, savior, deliverer, master, and God Almighty over every area of your life. What can God trust you with? Can he trust you with a ministry; can he trust you with a people group? Sometimes God's Word gets around us and begins to shake us so it can get inside and bear fruit in our lives. It cleanses us from old thinking. It cleanses us from religious activity back into real communion.

Matthew 11:29 says, "Take my yoke upon you. Let me teach you, because I am humble and gentle at heart, and you will find rest for your souls." He will give us rest. It doesn't say we will earn rest. This is a gift. It's not about earning—it's about positioning yourself. We take a seat of rest. Rest means total tranquility in the midst of chaos. Jesus knew how to rest. Everything must come out of rest; if you do it by striving or the work of your hands, it won't last. What we do is finite; what he does is infinite.

Hebrews 4:3 says,

> For only we who believe can enter his rest. As for
> the others, God said, 'In my anger I took an oath:
> They will never enter my place of rest,' even

though this rest has been ready since he made the world.

You have to first believe in the gift. Hebrews 4:9-11 says,

There is a special rest still waiting for the people of God. For all who have entered into God's rest have rested from their labors, just as God did after creating the world. Let us do our best to enter that rest. But if we disobey God, as the people of Israel did, we will fall.

Surrender to his Lordship so he can reign in your heart. Every heart has a throne. Who is sitting on the throne of your heart? You have to evict yourself out of the chair. We too often try to rescue ourselves. We also try to secure our futures, so we kick God out of the throne seat to drum up security when he has already mapped out a future for us. This is the struggle between self and Christ. Only one can reign in your heart at a time.

Rest is about your future. Surrendering and praying to God places your future safely in his hands. The key to understanding rest is understanding his heavenly government, his authority, and his function in your life. Jesus was at the greatest place of brokenness when the prayer, "Father, let this cup pass from me," gave the Father total authority over Jesus' life and future. He was surrendering to brokenness.

In the surrender, you will find peace. Peace is the ruler of rest. Stress will leave because peace and stress can't mix. We think our reward is in our wages, but they are just wages. Wages and rewards are different. Wages are about your labor; reward is about his gift. When your flesh is crying out for attention and glory, it's hard to stay in rest and peace. When the voices of doubt and stress plague you, point to Christ being on the throne of your heart and say, "Go take that up with Jesus." The voices will stay clear.

The labor is to go in. It's work. Deny the flesh. Deny your desires. Don't be consumed by what comes to you; only focus on what's coming out of you. There is a river that comes out of us. The Bible says out of your belly will flow rivers of living water. Rest releases the river of God through you into others. You will be full of the abundance of God so you will find yourself at the right place at the right time and connect with someone who needs the abundance of God flowing to them. This is called a *kairos* moment.

Rulership is all about the desire to serve the will of another. The enemy told Jesus he would give him rulership if he worshiped him. When you battle the enemy out of rest, the Lord is with you. When you do it by yourself, you get smashed. Rest will always bring dominion over chaos. Rest accomplishes more than striving ever could. God can do more in a moment of you resting in him than you can do in a thousand years of striving. You can receive this by doing it. It will bring divine alignment to your life. You will be more conscious of God's presence daily that comes to visit you. Ceaseless praying brings you to rest. When you have successfully prayed away your burdens, you get a seat in rest. The moment you leave that seat is when you fail to pray again once the thoughts of your old burden come knocking.

Rest is a magnet for heaven's activity. Rest will align your desires with God's desires. It won't be hard to engage God. You will remain a dead body but more alive in Christ than ever. This is being fully alive. Rest sets you apart because you're engaging a kingdom realm. While the world may be tortured by fear and turmoil, you are unmoved and seated in the unexplainable peace-filled seat of rest. Even if death knocks at your door, you are unmoved. You know that whatever may knock at your door, Jesus has the answer. If death, he is the resurrection; if sickness, he is healing; if turmoil, he is peace. The world cannot change or influence your life because you're engaged in Jesus. Rest also provides willful surrender to spending time with Jesus.

Here is a quote from American author Washington Irving:

> It is interesting to notice how some minds seem almost to create themselves, springing up under every disadvantage, and working their solitary but irresistible way through a thousand obstacles.[5]

When I had that nosebleed at Subway, it was likely the lowest point of my three-year season of sickness. The paramedics came and got the bleeding to finally stop. When I went home, I was exhausted and my stomach was hurting from drinking so much blood. I said, "God, am I going to die again? What if I go to sleep and bleed out?" I remember him saying, "John, you are being attacked by the devil. You better fast and pray! The next day I started fasting and praying. That was the end of that attack.

I continued to feel the draw to McKinney. It's almost like the Lord didn't consider me being sick when he was asking us to move. I prayed and looked for jobs there. One guy called because he was looking for a painter. I told him I was interested, and he came over to Shreveport for the interview. After meeting with him, I saw that the job seemed to be a good start. I told him I would take it. I shared with my mentors about it. One of them said to look for character. Little did I know I would find out there was very little of that with this new boss.

I gathered up my things to head to McKinney to begin work. Our house was still on the market, so I would be staying with a friend until we fully transitioned. This was total faith in Jesus healing me, knowing I had to provide for my family and I couldn't get sick at a new job. My first day at work, I worked a 16-hour day, painting cars. Shockingly, I didn't get sick one time. I ate what I wanted and painted cars. I wanted ice cream since I could eat freely again, but Bluebell wasn't producing due to bacteria in their factories. I was crazy excited! I couldn't believe I had been healed. I was blown away at God's love and power! Then I started thinking God wants to heal everyone!

I remember the Lord sharing the story of the lady that came to Jesus for healing:

> Jesus and his disciples got up and went with him. Just then a woman who had suffered for twelve years with constant bleeding came up behind him. She touched the fringe of his robe, for she thought, "If I can just touch his robe, I will be healed." Jesus turned around, and when he saw her he said, "Daughter, be encouraged! Your faith has made you well." And the woman was healed at that moment. (Matt. 9:19-22)

In Luke 17:14, "Jesus said to the man, stand up and go. Your faith has made you well." Only because of their faith in Jesus did these miracles happen. And Acts 3:16 says,

> Through faith in the name of Jesus, this man was healed—and you know how crippled he was before. Faith in Jesus' name has healed him before your very eyes.

As I adjusted to the new city and the new job, our house in Shreveport sold, so I went to pack the house and bring our things over to McKinney. Christine was eight months pregnant at this time, so it was rough on her to do a lot of physical work. I'm a very hyperactive human being, so it was no problem for me to unload the U-Haul and put stuff together.

We found a great apartment about five minutes from work. Just as we got settled in our new city, Christine began to go into labor. We were at a Super Bowl party when she felt the labor pains. We checked her into Baylor Hospital to begin the process of the delivery of our firstborn. Christine was in labor for 24 hours before we figured out that Deacon would not be a naturally born child. The doctor decided a C section was the best way to get him out. Afterward, Christine began to shake from all the medicine she had in her system.

When I first laid my eyes on Deacon, I got this feeling of fatherhood. The more I thought about it, the more I cried. I felt that I must take care of this baby at all cost. I was looking at my son, and it was one of my finest hours. He was very purple in color from the delivery process, so I walked over and rubbed his arm. As he cried, I put my finger in his little hand and calmed him down by speaking softly over him. I remember thinking about how much he would depend on me as his daddy. I was overwhelmed by emotions. That moment for me was life-changing. I felt a major sense of responsibility. I was made to be a daddy. I was made to be a husband. I was made to be a son.

We stayed at the hospital for about three days so Deacon could get all his tests done. Christine seemed to be recovering well, and I was thoroughly enjoying the benefits of being at Baylor Hospital. They brought me Starbucks coffee and pancakes every morning. I was impressed with their food and hospitality.

The day we left the hospital we had lasagna in a bag and all the baby stuff in another bag. As we arrived home, we were all ready to just sleep. Christine began to learn Deacon's sleep pattern, and I was learning how to be a new daddy. It is safe to say we had transitioned. Being new parents in a new city was difficult. Our family and friends made it happen, helping us on weekends with different tasks. Deacon didn't sleep very well by himself. He had to be in the bed with us, touching one of us. Christine didn't get much sleep at all.

As the months went by, we adjusted to our new normal. We found out it is rewarding to be parents. Christine and I both were so very thankful for the healing God had given me. We were also thankful for the precious gift he had given us in letting us be Deacon's parents.

As I bring this to a close, let's sit for a minute and reflect on how God has orchestrated all events for his good. I want to leave you with a few scriptures I have lived by since going through this season. I also want to thank you for reading this journey of healing. Please tell someone that God is a healer when you have the chance.

> O Lord, my God, I cried to you for help, and
>   you restored my health.
> You brought me up from the grave, O Lord. You
>   kept me from falling into the pit of death.
> (Psa. 30:2)

> You intended to harm me, but God intended it all
> for good. He brought me to this position so I
> could save the lives of many people. (Gen. 50:20)

> God uses all things to work together for the Good
> of those who love him and are called by his name.
> (Rom. 8:28)

---

[1] Jeremiah, Dr. David, *The Jeremiah Study Bible*, 19, Franklin: Worthy Publishing, 2013.

[2] Jesus Calling by Sarah Young, "There's no need to wonder whether or not you are going the right way," Facebook, September 30, 2019, https://www.facebook.com/JesusCalling/posts/theres-no-need-to-wonder-whether-or-not-you-are-going-the-right-way-i-am-the-way/10153457377743864/.

[3] Née, Watchman, *The Finest of the Wheat, Volume 2*, 139, New York: Christian Fellowship Publishers, Inc., 2014.

[4] "Trusting God with All Your Tomorrows by David Wilkerson," YouTube video, 49:06, "SermonIndex.net," April 10, 2014, https://www.youtube.com/watch?v=hEAEopnCzeM.

---

[5] Inspirational Quotes, "Overcoming Adversity Quotes," accessed September 20, 2019, http://www.inspirational-quotes.info/adversity.html.

www.ingramcontent.com/pod-product-compliance
Lightning Source LLC
LaVergne TN
LVHW041308080426
835510LV00009B/901